Note for Parents

GW01182737

How best can you help your child when they ask qu[...]d dying? Using simple, plain, language this book aims [...]e questions. Adults may find it difficult to talk about death and dying because of their own fears about the subject. However it is important for a child to feel that there are adults who are willing to listen to whatever they want to talk about and to answer their questions. Listening to a child's thoughts, beliefs and fears is the most useful way in which parents, teachers, carers and doctors can help children.

Sit and read this book with them; it may help with some of those difficult questions.

When someone dies

When someone we love dies we can feel very sad and want to cry, or feel scared and upset, or even angry. This can be the same whether you are a child or a grown up. If we know a bit more about death and dying, it can help us to understand and feel a little better.

This book covers some of the questions that you may want to ask a grown-up, doctor, teacher or friend when someone dies, and when you want to know what happens next.

Being alive and being dead

You are alive when you are reading this book. You can see the sights, hear the sounds, and touch, taste and smell, the things around you. It is not always like this though. Sometimes people stop being alive.

We know that plants die in winter. We know that animals die too. When people and animals and even plants stop being alive, we say they are 'dead' or they have 'died'. We accept this and understand that this is the way nature works. But it is much, much harder to understand why people have to die, especially someone we love very much.

Why do people have to die?

Dying is a natural part of life. All living things, plants, animals, and people die some day even though they all have a part to play in the world when they are alive. Nature usually allows most people to live long, happy and healthy lives.

When we say 'healthy', we mean that their bodies are working properly, breathing, moving and even when they're asleep. Just like a car needs to work properly to be able to drive on a road, our bodies need to stay working properly to keep us alive. But sometimes people die before they are old, because of an accident or illness. Something happens to them that they can't do anything about that makes their body go wrong and unable to work any longer. This is called death, or dying.

Does death hurt?

Doctors say that death doesn't hurt and we feel little pain. For very sick or very old people, it is like falling into a very deep sleep until they stop breathing and their heart stops beating. These people can be helped by special medicines that take away all the pain.

When someone dies in an accident, they often feel no pain at all because death happens so quickly. Very often they do not know what has happened so don't get frightened and don't suffer any pain. Many people who are sick or hurt and who know they are going to die even say that they feel calm and peaceful.

Why can't Doctors and Nurses stop someone from dying?

Doctors and Nurses in hospitals try their best to help all they can when someone is sick. Sick or injured people in hospitals are called 'patients'. Usually the doctors and nurses do make patients better so they can leave hospital and live long and healthy lives.

Because of new medicines people live much longer now than they did when our Grandparents were children. Sometimes, even though the doctors and nurses have tried their hardest, the patient dies. In this case, the doctors and nurses will have done their best to make sure that the patient is as comfortable and free from pain as possible.

Is death like sleeping?

People who are dead may look as if they are sleeping, but dying is nothing at all like being asleep. People and animals need sleep to rest and stay healthy. Sleeping allows your body time to rest and store up strength. While you are asleep you can dream and can wake up at anytime. When you wake up in the morning, you don't feel tired because your body has rested and is ready for another day.

When someone dies, their body stops working and they don't need to rest. They don't dream and they don't wake up because they no longer need their body. Their body is like an old car that has broken down and can't be driven any more.

How long will I live?

No one knows how long they will live, but most people live for a very long time. Think of how many old people you see every day. But no one lives forever, and if they did they would look very old indeed and the world would be overcrowded.

How long you will live depends on keeping fit, healthy and being careful. As we get older we learn more about growing older and dying, and we do not spend all our life worrying about it. You are much more likely to live a long, healthy life than to die young through an accident or illness, and so are your friends and family.

What happens to the person's body when they die?

When people die they don't need their bodies any longer and cannot feel pain anymore. We put their body in a box called a coffin, made especially for them. They are often taken to a place where they worshipped, such as a church, chapel, synagogue or mosque. Then we have a special service called a funeral where we can say goodbye to the person we love.

Mostly people are sad at funerals, as they didn't want their relative or friend to die. But sometimes at funerals we can also celebrate the fun and the good times we had when the person was still alive. You don't have to go to a person's funeral if you don't want to, but if you want to go, you can say goodbye to them one last time. There is usually music and people will say nice things about the person who has died.

Can I see the person who has died before the funeral?

When someone dies family and friends often go to a Funeral Home to see the person who has died so they can say goodbye before the funeral. The person who has died will be lying in a coffin. They will have their eyes closed and look as though they are asleep. You may want to talk to them as if they were still alive, say goodbye or even place a flower, card or drawing inside the coffin.

If you don't want to go to see them, you don't have to. If you feel worried about what it will be like, talk to a grown up about how you feel. You might want to wait and say goodbye at the funeral instead. It's your choice and if you don't go to see them it doesn't mean that you love them any less.

Where do dead people go?

Many people believe that when someone dies, part of that person lives on and goes to another place somewhere else. Christians call this place 'Heaven', Moslems call it 'Paradise' and other religions have their own special name. The part of us that people believe moves on after dying is not a bit of the body that you can point to like your head or your foot. It is the part of us that lets you feel love and happiness. It never gets sick and it never wears out. This part of us is called the spirit, or the soul.

Lots of people all over the world believe that when they die their spirits or souls live on. We cannot see someone's spirit and they cannot come back to visit us. We cannot see Heaven or Paradise either, but many people have faith in them. Faith means believing in something that we cannot see or hear.

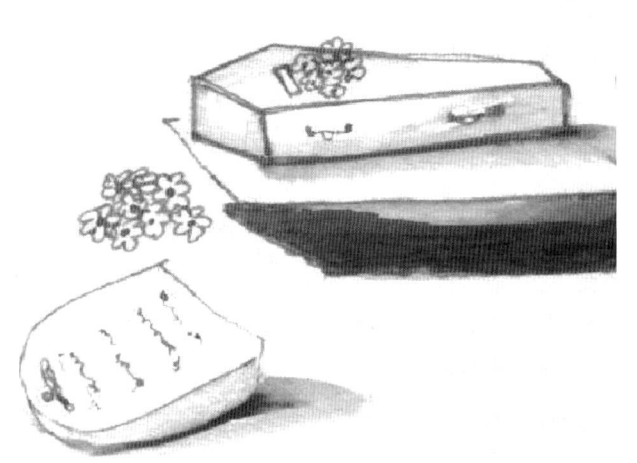

What happens after the funeral?

Just as the person who died doesn't need their body any longer, we don't need to see it to remember them so we find a special place to leave it. When the funeral service has finished, the coffin is taken to either a cemetery or a crematorium. A cemetery is a quiet place where we can come and think about the person we loved. Sometimes it is next to a church, or other place of worship.

In a cemetery, the coffin is put into a hole in the ground called a 'grave'. People at the burial each drop a bit of earth into the grave on top of the coffin as a special way of saying goodbye to the person who died.

A headstone or cross with their name on it will be put on their grave. When you visit the grave you can put flowers on it, and say a prayer for the person who has died if you wish to show that you still love the person.

Instead of being buried, some people are taken to a crematorium after they have died. Here their coffins are burnt and made into ashes. This is called 'cremation'. This doesn't hurt them as they cannot feel any pain. After the cremation, the ashes are put into a special jar or box. The ashes are then scattered somewhere peaceful, such as the gardens at the crematorium or another place that the person liked very much when they were alive. This might be their own garden or a place they used to visit a lot, sometimes even their favourite football ground.

Will I ever see the person who has died again?

When someone dies they cannot come back to their body again because it doesn't work any longer. You can't see or talk to that person again and that makes people very sad as they miss the person they loved. You may always miss them, but you won't always feel sad about it, you will in time be able to smile and laugh about the funny things you did together.

Your parents might have told you what they believe happens after we die. They will probably tell you that after you die yourself, you will meet up with all the friends and family members who died before you so you can all be together. That won't be for a long, long time, but meanwhile you can still love and remember the person who has died.

Why did someone I love very much have to die?

When someone you love dies, it seems very unfair. You may wonder why they had to die when you love them so much. It might be your best friend, cousin, brother or sister or your parent who has died and you don't know what you will do without them.

Almost everyone- it doesn't matter who they are or where they live - is loved by others. And almost everyone will be missed by others when they die. So whoever dies, someone will think it is very unfair and ask why it had to be that person. What is important is that you loved that person and that would have made them feel special.

When someone dies does it mean they are being punished?

We will all die one day and it makes no difference if you are good or bad. Many bad people live to an old age, but some nice people die young without ever doing anything horrible. Most people are given a wonderfully strong body that usually lasts a very long time.

Sometimes sickness or an accident makes them stop working before a person gets very old. This is not a punishment though. It just means that they were unlucky to get sick or to have an accident. Dying is never a punishment.

What if I have argued with the person who died?

You may feel very sad or guilty if you have argued or fought with someone just before they died. All these feelings are natural. Every young person has them. Most people can argue with others sometimes, but they still love each other.

Try and remember the fun you had with that person too. They probably loved being with you as much as you did with them. Even though their life was not as long as yours will be, it was mostly a happy life, because of the fun you had together.

Was it my fault they died?

When someone dies that you love, you might wonder if it was your fault, for being cross with them, or for being naughty. You might even think you could have stopped them from dying if only you'd done something different. Many grown ups think that too, but it isn't right.

You mustn't feel guilty if someone you love has died. You couldn't do anything to change it and it's not your fault.

Do people die because they are sad?

Being sad can make us feel sick sometimes, but very few people die because they are sad. Sometimes, when people have been together for a long time, if one of them dies it can make the other want to die too, so they can be back together again. This is when they need all the love and support they can get from their family and friends. That will help them feel better.

Can you think of times in the past when you were sad? Sooner or later you felt happy, you were able to smile and laugh again. Everyone goes through times like this; it has nothing to do with dying.

Why do people kill themselves?

Sometimes when people are very unhappy, sick or lonely they decide that they don't want to live any longer so they choose to die instead. This is called 'committing suicide'.

If someone you love does this it doesn't mean that they loved you any less. They might have wanted to stop you from suffering from their worries and problems. They might also have found it too hard to talk to other people about how they were feeling so no one and nothing would have been able to change this or stop them wanting to die.

Why do some children and babies die?

Sometimes, but not very often, babies and children die. A serious illness or a very bad accident can make this happen. This makes most people feel very unhappy. You might feel it isn't fair, and that the other child should have been able to have a long and happy life. You might think you will miss a friend, sister or brother more than you might miss anyone else.

Babies can be sick even before they are born, and maybe your parents were expecting a brother or sister for you but the baby was too ill to be born. That baby was a little person too and you and your family will still want to remember the baby even though you never got to see them.

How should I feel when someone dies?

You might feel sad, confused, angry, hurt, worried, tearful or lonely. You might not be able to believe that the person you love has died. Or you might feel numb, which means that you can't feel anything at all. All these feelings are natural and you might feel any or all of them at different times.

Sometimes you might feel like crying, so find a quiet place and let yourself cry. Grown ups do. Other times you might feel that you want to be happy and play, and this is alright too. Everyone is different, and has different feelings at different times. You might find it helps to talk to a grown up like a parent or teacher about how you feel. They might feel the same way too and you will be able to help each other, just by talking.

Why can't I sleep?

When someone you love has died, it is often very difficult to sleep. When you do go to sleep you might have dreams about the person where they are still alive. Other times you might get dreams that are a bit scary. It's so sad and frightening when someone dies that our minds have to work really hard to deal with it, and that's why bad dreams and sleeplessness happen.

If you can't sleep, or you've woken up because of a bad dream, don't worry about it because it is natural. Read a book or play with a favourite toy. Tell your parent so they know and can try to help you sleep better. In a little while you will be sleeping better again.

What will happen to me now?

If your parents have died, you will be very worried about what is going to happen to you. If you also have brothers or sisters you might also be afraid you will all be split up. A close relation, a grandparent, aunt or uncle will decide what will happen and will tell you.

Very few families ever want children to go and live with someone else or to be moved away from their brother or sister so they will look after you and love you. They might never be quite the same as a parent who died, but they will try their best to look after you and will give you a good home and love you.

How can I stop feeling so sad?

It is natural to cry and feel very sad when someone you love has died. You miss them, and you may feel lonely and confused too. Most people, grown ups and children, feel the same way when someone they love dies. Feeling sad is the same as feeling pain. It hurts a lot at first, and it's hard to think about anything else. But each day it hurts a little bit less, and some days it doesn't hurt at all.

One day the pain will be gone but that doesn't mean that you stop loving the person who died. Everybody feels sadness differently; sometimes you will be doing something you enjoy and you won't feel sad about the person who died. This is a good thing and you mustn't feel that you have to show you are sad all the time. The best thing is to find things to do that you enjoy, and also to talk to people about how you feel.

What can I do to help me feel better?

There are many things that you might like to do to help you when you are feeling sad about someone dying. You can write them a card or a letter, telling them how much you love and miss them, or things that you wanted to tell them but couldn't before they died. You can draw a picture of them, find little things that they liked or presents they gave you and collect these in a special 'memory box'.

Whenever you feel sad about them in the future, you can get the memory box out and think of all the happy times you had together. Above all, remember that you are still allowed to *be* happy when you *feel* happy. Tell your friends that you still want to see them and play with them, and that they mustn't be frightened to ask how you are feeling.

Why do the Police come to the house?

Unless someone dies in a hospital or at home after a long illness, the Police have to make sure everything is done properly. This doesn't mean that the person who died, or anyone else, did anything wrong.

The Police need to ask the family about the person who died, and what happened to them, so they can write a report. If the person died in an accident or a fight, they might need to make sure that the person who caused it is caught so they need to find out as much as possible from anyone who saw anything. The Police also want to try and make sure that the same thing doesn't happen to anybody else, so that other people don't have to suffer in the same way.

When I grow up will I understand more about death and dying?

As we grow up we learn more about many things including death and dying. We become used to seeing programmes on television and reading newspapers that tell us about people dying. This makes it easier to think about and talk about it.

The more we learn about life, the better we are able to understand the part of it we call death or dying. This means that when someone dies that we know and love, it is easier for us to deal with.